Distributed in the United States by
Smart Apple Media,
1980 Lookout Drive,
North Mankato,
Minnesota 56003

Text copyright © Linda Bygrave
Illustrations copyright © Louise Voce

Consultant: Michael Chinery

ISBN 1-93198-347-X
Library of Congress Control Number 2003102387

Printed in China

I am a
Crocodile

Written By
Linda Bygrave

Illustrated by
Louise Voce

Chrysalis Education

I am a crocodile.
I am big and strong with tough, scaly skin.

I have short legs, a long snout,
and a very toothy grin. Watch out!

My tail is very strong.

I swish it from side to side to swim fast.

I can run quite fast, too.

My eyes and nostrils are on top of my head.
When I swim through the water,
they are the only bits of me that show!

I like to live with other crocodiles.

We live beside lakes or rivers
in very hot countries.

In the morning I sunbathe.

If I get too hot, I open my mouth.

The air over my wet mouth cools me down.

I lie in the water at night to keep warm.
The hot sun warms the water by day,
so it is still warm at night.

These birds are picking bits of food
and leeches from my teeth.

This keeps my teeth clean . . . lovely!

I am a good hunter.

I eat anything I can catch.

I grab animals with my big teeth.

Then I twist round and round in the water
to tear off chunks of meat.

I am a mommy crocodile.
I look just like that daddy crocodile.

He is splashing and bellowing at me
because he likes me.
Together we will have some babies.

I am ready to lay my eggs.
First, I scrape out a nest
in the riverbank.

Then I lay about fifty eggs in the nest
and cover them with earth.
The earth helps to keep the eggs warm.

I protect my nest while my babies
are growing inside the eggs.

After ninety days my babies make a noise
that tells me they are ready to hatch.
I uncover the eggs to let them out.

I take my babies to the water.
I sometimes carry them in my mouth.
This keeps them safe.

They live in a special nursery pool.
There are holes in the riverbank
where they can hide.

I keep watch over my babies for about two months. They follow me around and climb over my snout and back.

They eat small things at first, like insects and worms. As they grow bigger, they eat bigger things

I have to keep my babies hidden. Big birds and lizards like to catch them for dinner!

I'm off to find a nice juicy bite to eat now . . .
Good-bye!